How to Read Anyone Instantly

----- ❧❧❧❧ -----

Discover the Secrets to Understanding Body Language, Master How to Analyze People with Psychology & Boost Your Success Without Saying a Word

Daniel Glanville

Your Free Gift

As a way of saying thank you for your purchase, I wanted to offer you a free bonus eBook called **5 Incredible Hypnotic Words to Influence Anyone.** Download the free guide here:
https://www.subscribepage.com/readanyone

If you're trying to persuade or influence other people then words are the most important tool you have to master.

As humans we interact with words, we shape the way we think through words, we express ourselves through words. Words evoke feelings and have the ability to talk to the reader's subconscious.

In this free guide, you'll discover **5** insanely effective words that you can easily use to start hypnotizing anyone in conversation.

Contents

Introduction

Iff you can analyze the people around you, you will be able to predict their future behavior, know what they're thinking, and be able to communicate in a precise and meaningful way with anyone you encounter. This is how important it is to be able to analyze someone. It gives you the power to negotiate social events, professional interactions, and even your relationships with confidence. It also provides you with the skills to know your mind and understand why you behave the way you do.

The book you now hold in your hand is a fast and effective way of being able to do all of this and much more.

By following the short chapters in this book, you will learn how to master psychological analysis in a short time. The sections of *How to Read Anyone Instantly* have been written in a way to provide you with only necessary information. We value your time and have striven to cut out filler, creating what we feel is a concise blueprint for success in the analysis of people. A blueprint you will be able to use in every aspect of your life to improve every personal marker for success significantly.

How to Read Anyone Instantly has been broken down into three sections, covering the origins of human

1

behavior; how to analyze body language, and how to understand human personality traits. Armed with the knowledge of all three, your new-found skills will empower you in being able to understand any individual on sight.

By reading this book, you will be taking your first and most crucial step into the world of decoding human behavior.

Part One

Human Behavior

Chapter 1
How to Analyze and Understand Behavior

Before we get into a detailed overview of analyzing people and their behaviors, you need to have a solid understanding of the basics. That's what this chapter is all about - providing a foundation about behavior which will help you attain mastery in reading people on sight. But don't worry, it'll be fun - I promise. Let's get to it!

What is Behavior, and Where Does it Come From?

A person's behavior can be broken down into three main categories:

1. Their actions.
2. Their speech.
3. Their nonverbal communication.

Essentially, behavior is anything a person does, which affects the world and the people and things within it.

1. Your actions are your physical interactions with the world.
2. Your speech is anything you say and the way you say it.
3. Nonverbal communication covers facial expressions and the way you present your body, such as hand gestures, posture, and eye contact, etc.

These three types of behavior all involve *communication*. They speak to observers, letting them know what someone is like as a person.

There is an essential fourth form of behavior which is often overlooked, and we will touch upon this later. This fourth category is what you *don't* do. You see, every inaction is, in fact, an action. If you decide not to eat those six doughnuts when everyone around you is stuffing their face, this shows that you have self-control and are potentially a more disciplined person.

Combined together, any individual's behavior can be used to understand:

*   What they want.
*   The content of their character.
*   To predict their future behavior.

When you gain mastery in how to read people on sight, you will quickly be able to do all three of these things, just by observation. This skill will transform how you interact with people.

Why Do We Do What We do?

To analyze someone properly, you need to be able to weigh up which behaviors are more dominant than others. People are complex and often contradictory. How many people do you know are capable of being incredibly kind, but also mean? If you can decide which behaviors an individual is likely to carry out, you will predict their behavior more accurately. How likely are they to be kind vs. mean? Of course, this is a gross simplification. Still, as you and I journey through this book, you will develop a robust understanding of how to weight up behaviors.

Not only is weighing up the likelihood of a given behavior significant, but it's also critical that you know the source of behavior to understand its power and nature. In psychology and philosophy, there is a great debate over the cause of our actions. Some believe that the genes produce behaviors we inherit from our parents. In contrast, others argue that we learn our practices from the environment in which we are brought up. It is often called the nature/nurture debate. Is your personality, a result of your behavior, genetic (nature), or the environmental (nurture)?

Over the last twenty years or so, we have developed a greater understanding of our genetics and how they impact us. It has bolstered a third view that behaviors are a mix of *both* nature and nurture. A gene can be associated with being more aggressive, for example, and another gene more passive. However, evolution has given us a neat trick. The power of *epigenetics*. It merely means that we can switch any gene on or off. It allows us to adapt to our environment. So, for example, let's say a person grows up to be an athlete. No one in their family is athletic, but a coach encouraged this individual when they were young to train and run faster. Their body would adapt over time, and so too would their behavior! As they push their body in training, the genes influencing muscle growth would switch on or become more dominant.

Neural pathways are another way our biology and experiences combine to create our behaviors. These pathways are connections between cells in the brain called neurons. As we learn things, these connections grow stronger. If you learn to play the piano, you'll develop a vast network of connections between specific neurons that carry, not just the memory of being able to play, but also the muscle memory, music theory, rhythm, and reaction times all needed to play. It is the same with any behavior. Have you ever found it difficult to form a new habit, such as working out or studying enough? It takes time for those neuronal pathways to strengthen enough that your behavior becomes almost automatic. In essence, you don't need to think about it anymore; you just do it. It is a fantastic interplay between biology (your brain) and your environment (which your brain reacts to).

We can see then that the behaviors we have are this incredibly complex combination of the genes we have, our experiences switching genes on and off which give us better abilities, and pathways in the brain are growing out of our environment.

And so, it isn't quite nature vs. nurture, but instead: Our behavior is *nurtured by nature*.

What Does my Behavior Display?

Is a person their behavior? It isn't an easy question to answer. Still, it's an important one to explore to understand what can actually be learned about a person from the way they behave. In the film *Batman Begins*, the Dark Knight himself says, *"It's not who I am underneath, but what I do that defines me."* For Batman, he doesn't have to be a billionaire playboy Bruce Wayne by day, what matters most is what he contributes when he puts on the cowl and cape at night.

I don't use this example just because I'm a massive comic book fan - it's an important concept when analyzing people. What does your behavior say about you? Simplistically, if you give money to the poor, does that make you a good person? What if you beat someone up to get that money? You've both done an evil thing and a good thing. Which one are you, good or bad?

People are complicated, and as I said previously, we often contradict our actions. We're also capable of redeeming our "bad" behaviors with good ones. And so, a person isn't entirely their behavior, because they can change that behavior over time. They may also do something out of character. Instead, it's more accurate to see a person's *current* practice as a snapshot of who they are at a specific time. Though people do change, it tends to be over a long period, so if you can analyze that snapshot, you can understand who they are, what they want, and how they are likely to act in the *short term*, maybe even the long term if they don't change their way of thinking.

But what sort of things does your behavior and the behavior of others say about them at that moment?

How to Use Different Techniques to Analyze Behavior

As we said at the beginning of this chapter, there are three main types of behavior, which include physical actions, what someone says and how they say it, and nonverbal communication, also known as body language. The techniques for analyzing behavior must be designed to gather information from these three areas (the fourth behavior of *inaction* requires a different skill set, which we'll expand upon later).

Let's take a broad look first at some techniques which are useful to any self-respecting master of analysis.

Introspection

Before Psychology was founded as a discipline, there was a group of people called the introspectionists. These forerunners to modern psychology believed that they could learn everything about people in general by analyzing their thoughts and feelings, and how those thoughts determined their behaviors. Though science has built on their work to make psychology more objectively based and consistent, the process of introspection is still a powerful one. It allows a person to think about how they feel and behave, and then apply any conclusions to others. We do have a shared humanity, after all.

For example, let's say you got angry at a friend and insulted them. An introspectionist would ask:

1. Why did I feel angry?
2. Why did I then react to the anger in that way?

You might conclude that your friend wasn't in the wrong and that you felt defensive about something. You might then be able to trace this back to an event that happened before. Maybe you were angry at your friend about something else, and that dormant anger came out at the wrong moment. Perhaps you were stressed about other things and irritable. There are a million and one reasons, but through introspection, we can learn about the process of going from a feeling to an action, whether physical, verbal, or nonverbal.

You can then look for similar behavior in others, and often you'd be right that they are experiencing the same thing. Self-knowledge through introspection is extremely powerful, but care must be made to back this up with other techniques below to disprove or verify your conclusions.

Observation

Another essential technique is to observe a person's behavior like a detective, tracing their practice back to a source feeling or thought. Let's say you're talking to a business competitor about their business. When you mention their social media campaigns, the competitor folds her arms and leans back slightly. She also becomes less amiable. You've hit a nerve. Could it be that her social media campaign isn't going very well? Or perhaps it's going very well, and she's afraid you'll copy her approach? By observing a person's behavior closely and always asking, *"what are they thinking?"* and *"what does their body language, speech, and actions mean?"* you can gain great insight into a person's thought process and future decisions.

Reaction

How does a person make you feel? What's your intuition about them? Are you immediately distrustful of them? Or do you feel happy in their company? Never dismiss your gut instinct. The reason for this is that your emotional reaction to someone is based on the subconscious processing of a person's behavior. You might encounter someone, and they are smiling and saying all the right things, but deep down, you feel they are insincere, and you don't know why. There's a good chance that your subconscious mind has heard something off in their speech or seen something unusual yet subtle in their facial expressions, perhaps their eye contact, that is telling you to *be careful.* Of course, you don't want to be overly distrustful, and so you should return to introspection and ask yourself why you are feeling the way you do. If you can lock into what your subconscious is picking up about an individual, you will develop the skill of reading people much faster.

Reading Between the Lines

When we explore the three techniques we've just mentioned in greater detail, you will learn how to read between the lines. That saying comes from literature analysis. If you take an author's fictional words literally, you miss the subtext and depth which is hidden within. That's what is contained *between the lines*.

In the same way, when you learn to observe and interpret body language, speech, and actions, you will be able to read between that person's behavior to what's underneath. You'll achieve mastery in understanding who a person is, why they are behaving the way they are, and what they are likely to do in the future. It's like a superpower, plus you don't need to defeat an evil villain wielding a gigantic laser to become good at it, which is always a bonus.

And what will that mastery give you?

- It would give you the ability to make deeper connections with your loved ones, both present, and future, by understanding how they're feeling and by appropriately reacting to this.

- It would give you the skillset to negotiate business deals, competition, and staff interactions with confidence.

- It will allow you to become a better and more productive human being by being able to interact with individuals and groups, empowered with the codex to unlock people's true feelings and desires.

Chapter 2
The Limbic System and Behavior

To understand how to analyze and predict behavior, we must develop a solid understanding of where behavior comes from. In this chapter, we are going to look at the limbic system as one component of behavior. Once we understand this system, we will be able to better decode our behavior and the behavior of others.

You Have More Than One Brain

In some sense, we do indeed have more than one brain. That said, we have different neurological systems that, when isolated, tend to process and produce specific information. We can conceptualize these structures as their processing units, or brains, which can help us understand what each area does. In terms of behavior, this is an important distinction, as some of these structures compete with each other for dominance. Whenever we experience cognitive dissonance - the uncomfortable feeling of two competing ideas - we are experiencing these different "brains" or systems trying to produce their own behaviors. In this sense, we really are a colony of behavioral systems crying out to be heard.

In a broad sense, we can break down our behaviors into two systems in the brain:

- The limbic system
- The prefrontal cortex

The limbic system is a conglomeration of structures that deals with raw, primitive emotional feelings and behaviors. The prefrontal cortex is influenced by this system. It can funnel or override these emotions and desires through rational thought, decision making, and problem-solving.

In this chapter, we are primarily interested in the limbic system.

Understanding the Limbic System

The limbic system is comprised of several structures. However, we want to primarily focus on the hypothalamus, the hippocampus, and the amygdala, as these are the key influencers on human behavior. They are fundamentally responsible for creating a person's emotional life and sense of self.

Hypothalamus: This structure creates homeostasis in a person's mind. It means to bring the world back into balance. For example, to regulate impulses concerned with hunger, thirst, pleasure, sexual desire; along with primitive emotions like anger. The hypothalamus seeks to quench an inclination one way or another. If you're hungry - eat. If you're aroused - have sex. If you're angry - lash out or vent.

Hippocampus: This structure is primarily concerned with converting the "here and now" with the past and the future. It allows a person to create new memories, placing meaning and weight on people, things, and events. It can significantly affect behavior. For example, if you met someone who angered you, you may record that memory and decide to either avoid that person in the future or confront them after the fact.

Amygdala: This structure deals with arousal, aggression, and fear. It helps produce behaviors dominated by these three components and often mixes them. A fearful response can result in a defensive attack, for example. When this structure is damaged, individuals become incredibly passive. Still, they can also lack a standard fear response, which can be dangerous. If your amygdala tells you that a busy road is dangerous, you are less likely to cross it. If your amygdala is damaged, you may walk out into traffic without realizing the danger.

All three structures within the limbic system combined help produce and cause emotional states, which can lead to impulsive behaviors. Their output can then also be sent to the prefrontal cortex, which might, through rational thought and forward planning, decide not to act out one's deepest desires for fear of repercussions. It can, in some way, divide a brain into two, fighting for your attention.

How the Limbic System Helps You to Deal with Threats

Understanding the human response to a perceived threat is essential to analyzing behavior. A "threat" in this sense does not have to be something physically dangerous. However, it probably evolved out of a neural system, which primarily dealt with that. A threat can be anything from the risk of peer opinion, loneliness, insecurity, to the danger of aggression. We can think of threat as being anything which creates a feeling of uncertainty to oneself. It could be something that threatens your sense of self-worth, your emotional happiness, or your physical body.

You may have come across the term "fight or flight" reflex, in classic psychology, there are three primal responses to perceived threats produced by the limbic system: freeze, fight, and flight. A fourth is also sometimes included, "fuck", though this reflex is a little more controversial. All four reflexes have evolved to allow you to survive a threat, whether to survive emotionally or to survive physically.

Let's take a look at the three which are most established in the scientific literature. If you have ever felt paralyzed by fear or have experienced feeling like you are waiting for something during a threat, this is your limbic system asserting itself. In a physical confrontation, this would involve either playing dead or merely ceasing to fight back. In a psychological encounter, this would be not saying anything in response or acting out.

The freeze reflex is very common; however, its strength will depend on a person's genetics and their experiences. A person who has been badly hurt in a previous physical attack may have a reduced freeze reflex, or they may have a strengthened one if previously fighting back resulted in more harm than good. Likewise, freezing in response to someone psychologically will stop you from saying or doing something rash. Still, it could also prevent you from acting when you should.

Fight Response

The fight response is self-explanatory. It is when, in response to a threat, a person ramps up their aggressive behavior. It could be physically lashing out or verbally shouting at someone. However, it does not always have to be so overt. For example, the fight response could help someone stand up to a bully at work or school, without having to resort to either physical or verbal assaults. The fight response can push a person onward when faced with difficult hurdles. Still, it can also overreach and cause a person to become violent or make mistakes, trying to be proactive.

Flight Response

The flight response or reflex switches a person's brain into pattern recognition mode. Instantly, the person is looking at their surroundings and trying to find a way out of a situation. It could be running away from a physical fight, but it could also be detaching from a marriage or friendship. Some people have very dominant flight responses, and so when life gets complicated, they often check out from their commitments or quit a task at the first hurdle. It can, however, also save your life.

Fuck Response

This contentious response is sometimes included in psychology textbooks. It involves sexual arousal and resultant behavior. Whether it is due to a threat response, it is debatable. However, some believe that when faced with death, that there is an evolutionary response to breed. One example of this was during and after World War II when there was a boom in births. Other threats could include copulation with another person's partner to undermine them or protect your social status.

How the Limbic System Helps You to Recover from Threats

The responses previously mentioned all combine to create most of the human behaviors we display as a species. They bubble up from this cauldron of competing feelings, desires, and decisions. This conglomeration of beliefs can result in an internal struggle of impulses, which in turn can cause anxiety and nervousness. More than this, as human beings, we have to have the exact mechanisms to be able to weather the storm of our emotions and bring ourselves back to a healthy state. It is another example of homeostasis in action.

And so, if we look at the limbic system as several structures, which process information and produce emotions and drives in response, we can also see it as an intervener of sorts. The limbic system has ways to calm itself and you. These manifest as behaviors, movements, and even in extreme cases, complex obsessive rituals, which ease the mind and soothe our anxieties. These behaviors are known as "adapters".

Type of Adapters You Need to Know

By being able to identify adapters, you will have the power to not only soothe your inner feelings but also be able to see when others are comforting themselves as well. When you spot an adaptive behavior, you will instantly know that a person is experiencing powerful emotions or an anxious state of mind. It, in turn, will help you explain their behavior should they seem on edge. At best, you will be able to anticipate their nervousness and be able to either help them alleviate this through interactions or be able to prepare yourself defensively for any negative behaviors carried out by the individual as a result of these impulses.

Let us quickly take a look at some common adapters for you to use and observe in others.

Touching or Stroking the Neck

This adapter involves rubbing or touching the back of the neck with one hand. It is sometimes referred to as the "pain in the neck posture" because it is the same action someone might carry out if they were experiencing actual pain in the neck. This pain can also indicate that someone, something, or even an event is a figurative pain in the neck and consequently causing frustration. It can also infer that a person is experiencing anger. This behavior should be seen as an indicator that a person is controlling or holding back their negative emotions. They are keeping things in check. It is also used to imply that the individual is considering a frustrating situation, even thinking up a solution.

If the front of the neck is being touched instead, then this is more indicative of nervousness. The neck is an extremely vulnerable body part, which contains the windpipe and jugular veins. Subconsciously, when we feel under threat, we attempt to guard or protect our most sensitive body parts. It again is a by-product of evolution and shows the overlap between physical vulnerability and psychological vulnerability.

Touching or Stroking the Face

The face is our primary means of nonverbal communication, but how we treat our faces can also imply our state of mind. It involves stroking or touching the face in different ways. It may partly be a learned behavior. Parents will often feel the faces of their children and infants in an affectionate way, which can be naturally calming. Touching your face may be a way to emulate this sensation and self soothe. It is for this reason that nervousness or stress often brings about this adaptive behavior.

Other examples which can mean different things include the face platter - a courtship gesture, usually by females, when looking at a prospective mate and resting their chin on their hands, with their elbows on their thighs or a table. Another face touching behavior such as the single or double facepalm can denote shock or frustration.

Whistling

You have no doubt seen this behavior in old cartoons. Whenever a character has done something terrible, and they want to act as though they had nothing to do with it, they will often whistle loudly and walk away as if relaxed. Whistling sits in a grey area as it is a sound, but still processed usually as nonverbal communication. What makes reading whistling difficult is that it is genuinely used by some people when they are happy. For some people, it is a genuine expression of relaxation, while others will whistle to soothe themselves and/or signal to those around them that they are calm when internally they are not.

An excellent way to spot when whistling is being used during an awkward moment is if there are momentary breaks in the whistle. In those moments, the individual loses focus and internally goes over their negative emotional desire. It is a real giveaway but is not always present. It should also be remembered that whistling can be used to self-motivate and make a task more bearable.

Leg Cleansing

Also known as Leg Pacifying Behavior, this particular adapter involves touching or rubbing your legs, usually your thighs. This action can soothe an individual and promote the release of calming neurotransmitters. It also allows a nervous individual to calm sweat, which often occurs in the palm of their hands. This type of self-touching can have a negative impact on observers, as it telegraphs discomfort and perspiration. It is for this reason that it is a good idea to use this adapter out of sight. Leg cleansing often comes in tandem with other low confidence or agitated body language cues, such as those mentioned above.

Part Two

Body Language

Chapter 3
Understanding Body Language: The Basics

Having established the importance of the limbic system in creating behavior and seeking out homeostasis, we can now open up to a broader exploration of body language. Understanding how we use and interpret body language is a vital part of reading people and adapting to the potential psychological states of other individuals.

What is Body Language and Why Is It So Important?

It is likely that you already have a good understanding of what body language is, but let us define it more strictly, so we are on the same page. Also referred to as "nonverbal communication", body language includes any physical movement, action, or pose, which conveys meaning. This language can be broken down into two categories:

Conscious: Deliberate nonverbal movements and poses, which are used by an individual to communicate a feeling or desire.

Unconscious: Internal feelings that individuals try to keep hidden, and nonetheless, find expression through postures and movements, which lead to the person being so unaware of, that they do not control them.

As a result, body language is an expression of both the conscious and unconscious mind.

How Does Body Language Reveal Your Emotions and Thoughts?

From the day a person is born, they become pattern-seeking and meaning attributing beings. This two-part process simply means that we automatically look for deliberate or consequential patterns in the world around us, and then interpret those events by assigning meaning to them. A simple example of this would be a person frowning. Our brains see this facial pattern of muscle movement. Then we attribute an interpretation to it - in this case, the person seems sad.

Body language is simple as a concept; however, the interpretation of it and understanding of the mechanisms at play are more complex. Interpretation, it must be remembered, is always open to subjectivity, and therefore there is still room for error. That being said, there are several established body language components that researchers have reliably isolated as having a specific meaning.

As we have established, there are different structures in the brain, competing with each other for dominance. We have also found that body language comes in both conscious and unconscious forms. When intentional communication through nonverbal postures and movement is in effect, the competing structures tend to agree with each other. For example, individuals feeling anger may then take up a dominant position, which includes a fixed stare, standing taller, puffing the chest out, and maintaining a serious expression in the face. All of this is used to tell a person, *"I'm dangerous, back off! Don't push me too far, or I won't respond in kind."* It is a conscious body language. It's crucial here to recognize that these behaviors may be automatic, that is, the person is not consciously controlling every single component of the body language. Instead, think of it as a gate. When the barrier is consciously lifted, the body language contained is released.

But what about unconscious body language? In this instance, the gate is consciously closed. The individual, for example, maybe feeling anger, resentment, even hatred. However, he or she does not want anyone to know they are feeling this way. The gate is closed, and the body language which would communicate these aggressive feelings is hopefully kept contained. Think of a professional situation, for example. If you were feeling angry at your boss, you might want to curtail those feelings, as acting on them could result in being fired. In this instance, you have consciously closed the gate. You are trying to calm yourself down to reach homeostasis or using the adapters that we mentioned in the previous chapters to vent and alleviate these feelings.

This, however, does not always work. When it comes to body language, the components which deeply desire to be known can push through holes in the gate. When this happens, no matter how hard you try, some evidence for how you genuinely feel will present itself. You might consciously smile and act as though you are not angry; however, your eye contact may betray your true feelings, or perhaps you may cross your arms, taking up a defensive stance.

Body language can affect our communication profoundly. It can manifest consciously and unconsciously because the competing structures in the brain produce components of emotion, which want to be known regardless of your conscious intentions. If you understand this principle and know what to look for, you can better understand and anticipate what a person is thinking and how they are going to act. It can also give you an advantage when trying to keep the gate closed, becoming aware when your inner desires and behaviors seep out and responding to curtail them.

Universal Gestures

Let us now take a broad look at some universal gestures which have been identified by psychologists as conveying a person's real state of mind. We can break these gestures down into three main categories:

Body Proxemics: These gestures involve how an individual moves their body in space. Hand, leg, and arm gestures are the most common. How a person holds their head can also communicate meaning, along with a person's stance and how they are leaning.

Facial Expression: This is the primary communication method human beings use outside of language. As babies, we respond naturally to specific facial expressions, implicitly decoding them. When a person feels an intense emotion, their facial expression becomes more pronounced. Still, even those who have mastery over their outward appearance will give subtle facial cues about their inner feelings.

Ornaments: Body language is not just about how we move our bodies and our faces, but also how we interact with the world around us. Clothing, hairstyles, jewelry, tattoos, these can all be ways for a person to convey who they are and what they think. However, it is often in how they touch and handle objects, such as jewelry, where the most significant insight can be learned.

In later chapters, we will discuss specific examples of each, illustrating how you can use these to master communication.

10 Golden Rules to Master the Art of Deciphering Common Body Language

Now that we have established what body language is, how it affects our behavior, and what the primary forms of body language are, we should now look at ten essential rules for interpreting body language. Throughout the rest of this book as you learn specific key components to body language, always keep these ten rules in mind. They will provide a guide for you when interacting with others and trying to read their body language.

Don't read individual gestures: Body language interpretation is open to subjective reading and, therefore, error. As an interpreter, it is essential to minimize the chance of failure as much as possible. To do this, you mustn't put too much weight on one single piece of nonverbal communication. Look at the other gestures a person is using to create a more holistic impression of their thoughts.

Search for harmony: If we look at body language holistically, we create a more detailed impression of what a person is thinking. Once we do that, we should then look for patterns. Is there an agreement between those gestures? It is a search for harmony. Look at all the individual pieces of body language and try to find the most significant number conveying the same feeling.

Read gestures in context: Context is king. Always take into account the environment, past events, and future events. Someone who has just argued might seem defensive or angry, but that does not necessarily mean that they are mad at you. Likewise, someone might be anxious about a future event such as an exam, that does not mean that they are concerned about where they currently are. The environment can also play tricks. Someone might have their arms folded, not because they are defensive, but because they are cold. They might even frown because they cannot hear properly over loud music, but that does not mean that they are angry.

Recognize and decipher quirky nonverbal cues: While there are broad, standard body signals, everyone has their quirks. One individual might laugh or smile when they are nervous, while another might become stoic and straight-faced. Over time, look for these quirks and try to understand them within the context of the unique individual you are analyzing.

Try to establish baseline behaviors: People are complicated; however, we can broadly speak, place people into specific personality categories. It is why psychometric data is so powerful in psychology. Someone might be more passive naturally, while another more assertive. Once you know what "kind" of personality a person has, you can establish this as a baseline. Then, you can look for what is out of the ordinary, evaluating temporary changes to this baseline.

Study behavioral changes that could lead to a shift in the decision: Sometimes, people will do a 180 turn on any given decision. It can sometimes go against the grain of who they are usually. However, body language can betray this uncertainty. Look for indecision in their demeanor. It is commonly seen in a furrowed brow, with the eyes staring to the side or upwards as they think over what to do. It can also be seen as a defensive stance transitioning to an aggressive one as they are empowered by changing tact. So, look for a closed-off posture turning to a "puffed chest" and broad-shouldered position.

Watch out for misleading nonverbal clues: Deception is a primal human behavior. We all do it in one form or another, whether little white lies or huge, life-changing secrets. Read body language with suspicion. Think about what seems conscious and unconscious. Someone may be smiling, but their posture may show they are far from happy. Look for this deception and use this understanding to discover what a person is honestly thinking.

Distinguish between comfort and discomfort: We can fit most body language signals into two categories of comfort or discomfort. It is a quick road to figuring out where a body signal comes from. If it is discomfort, it is harmful; if it is comfortable, it is positive. Then ask yourself, why is this person comfortable or uncomfortable?

Don't act like a creep when analyzing people: In science, especially psychology, we have to be wary of the observer effect. It is a universal truth that when measuring something, the very act of measurement changes what you are trying to measure. It is also true when analyzing body language. Stay natural and make measurement subtle. If it is obvious you are staring and not listening to a person, their body language will change in response, muddying the waters and making it harder to distinguish between behaviors brought about by your observations and those which were already there.

Understand what you see through fluid thinking: Be open to change. Body language and other forms of non-verbal communication are complex. If you feel sure that one way of non-verbal communication is indicative of a specific thought or motive, do not apply this with 100% confidence at all times. There will be times where you are required to shift or alter the meaning you attribute to an instance of non-verbal communication. Do not stick to your guns regardless of the data. Think about what you are seeing. Put it in the context of the environment and what is happening around you. Use a fluid problem-solving approach and do not be afraid to discard a conclusion if the evidence calls for it. Communication is fluid, and so must be your interpretation skills.

Why Do We Misread People?

We continually seek these two aspects of pattern recognition and then meaning attribution. However, if we develop the skill of reading body language throughout life, why do we find ourselves in situations where we misread someone's intentions or poorly predict their future behavior? Reasons for this include:

Subjectivity: What we deem significant body language is very person-centric. It is often based on how important we feel behavior is. If we, for example, find facial expressions to be more meaningful than body language, then we might ignore body signals. What we naturally think of as remarkable is usually a product of our genetics and our past experiences, so this creates a lot of room for error when applying our outlook onto the inner thoughts of another person, who may think very differently from us.

An extreme example of this would be someone who has an antisocial behavior personality disorder. It is sometimes classified as psychopathic. They would experience the world in a very different way from the average person, and so reading their body language is far more difficult due to high levels of deception.

Cognitive Processing: The truth is, observing body language consciously takes brain resources. This cognitive processing is not as easy as only taking a person's verbal communication at face value. Our brains often strive to achieve a goal with the least amount of effort; this saves energy. When we do this, we ignore or overlook nonverbal communication.

Deception: As already stated, we are natural deception machines. We develop this trait as infants when we realize other people see the world differently from us, and that we can change their perception by picking which information we share with them. New research indicates that babies as young as six months may have the ability to deceive, though it is most prevalent between 3 and 6 years of age. As adults, we hone this ability, and so some can control their body language better than others to deceive.

Poor Interpretation Skills: Often, we simply have not developed the skills to correctly interpret body language and other forms of nonverbal communication effectively. Take when a person is talking. If someone does not look you in the eye, you may conclude they are lying, but it could also be that they are just nervous. We often also assume the same when someone pauses to say *"uh"* during a speech. It can be a sign that they are having to think through what they are saying because they are lying, but it also could be that they are naturally nervous.

The Trick to Becoming an Effective Reader

When we try to understand what nonverbal communication says about a person's thoughts and future potential actions, we can think of ourselves as a detective. Another word for it would be "decoders". We are presented with coded information, especially when it is unconscious body language. We must then decipher the data and interpret the clues given. Like any skill, this takes practice, but people who dedicate their time to it can achieve mastery. This mastery significantly improves the way an individual can communicate, predict, and strategize when conversing with others.

Ways to improve reading skill involve:

Awareness: Any complex ability requires a substantial amount of brainpower initially. You must focus on the task and think through each step. Eventually, this skill then becomes ingrained and becomes mostly automatic. Developing an awareness of body language and thinking about this will create this automatic skillset.

Patience: Do not beat yourself up if you make mistakes. Even the most seasoned "mind readers" have errors, simply because people are so deceptive and variable. The trick is to remain patient and understand that you will improve over time.

Adaptability: If we conclude early on in interaction about what kind of a person someone is and their resulting behavior, this can severely limit our ability to read them adequately. Remember, people have quirks; they also change their minds based on their personality and the context they are operating within. Always be open to changes and new information. Never be afraid to reappraise your conclusion.

Listen to Your Instincts: It is essential to acknowledge that you already have *some* skill in reading body language. Unless you have a learning, difficulty which impedes this, you have already implicitly learned to process a person's nonverbal communication subconsciously. Listen to these feelings. As mentioned in a previous chapter, you will find yourself in situations where something seems "off" about an individual. Listen to this and observe their body language. Ask yourself if it is in line with what they appear to be saying or doing. Be open-minded; your gut may be wrong, so also look for evidence which refutes your instinct. In this situation, do what Socrates always advised - follow the evidence wherever it leads.

How to Influence Others Through Your Body Language

In the upcoming chapters, we will dive into all the different types of nonverbal cues you should look for in others, but remember that these can also be applied to yourself. Through knowledge of how nonverbal communication affects others, and through observing your nonverbal cues, you can change the way you act to convey leadership, strength, and even vulnerability when needed.

Chapter 4
Verbal Vs. Nonverbal Communication

Now that we have established a good foundation for becoming a competent reader of body language, we will place this in the context of overall communication. What we mean by this is that nonverbal and verbal communication come together as a package. They can "say" different things, but to understand a person's thoughts and intentions, we have to perceive all the ways they are trying to communicate. Imagine a person smiling as they verbalize a threat. If we do not pay attention to the content of the person's speech, then the smile seems harmless. If, however, we place their smile in the context of the verbal threat, then it becomes a menacing smile and conveys something entirely different.

Essentially, we need to understand both verbal and nonverbal communication as ways to communicate, which often overlap and sometimes disagree. Once we understand both together, we can then indeed decode what a person is thinking.

Daniel Glanville

What is Verbal and Nonverbal Communication?

Simply put, verbal communication is anything that is spoken. However, the communication *must contain words*. Nonverbal communication involves body language, facial expressions, and gestures. It also includes vocalizations such as grunts, whistling, musical humming, and any other vocal noise which does not contain language.

Similarities Between Verbal and Nonverbal Communication

Both verbal and nonverbal communication contain meaning. They also convey this meaning to the outside world, sometimes consciously and sometimes subconsciously. We have spoken about how nonverbal communication can appear even when a person is trying to stop it. This unintended form of communication is powerful, and it is also why readers of body language can know so much about people from their physical postures and gestures.

Verbal communication has a similar subconscious component. We call this *subtext*, and we briefly mentioned this in a previous chapter. The subtext is the hidden message found in the words people use and how they say them. A person could give a compliment, but their tone could be sarcastic or mocking. Such subtext can be subconscious, where the true meaning of someone's words seeps through even when not intended. Likewise, sometimes a person can use language and tone to convey a meaning deliberately. For example, let us say you are late for a meeting with a business client. When you arrive, you apologize, and the business client uses the words *"it's fine."* However, their tone is one of annoyance. These verbal clues can key you into what someone is thinking.

And so, we can see then that both verbal and nonverbal communication share much in that they communicate meaning, and can do so consciously or subconsciously. General analysis of both can be said to have the same aims then - to decode that meaning.

Differences Between Verbal and Nonverbal Communication

While decoding both verbal and nonverbal communication has the same broad aims, how we do this decoding is markedly different. The reason for this is that despite both being mediums for communication, they present what a person is thinking in different ways.

The most crucial key distinction is that because nonverbal communication does not use "words" as part of its language, we, therefore, must use a higher level of scrutiny when trying to decode what a person's nonverbal communication is saying. It means that there is a far greater chance of error, which is why it is essential to look at what a person is saying. Also, observe several different parts of their nonverbal communication to try to verify the meaning.

Verbal communication is also much faster. When we enter into a conversation, a large amount of information can be exchanged over a short space of time. Because of this, verbal shifts in meaning happen quickly. However, nonverbal communication tends to work much slower. Feelings slowly seep to the surface and present as posture changes, facial expressions, and gestures. All of this can change in the course of a conversation. However, the presentation of information happens at a much slower rate.

Perceptions: Having a Better Understanding of How We Interpret Verbal and Nonverbal Communication

When we think about the two types of *conscious* and *subconscious* (unconscious) communication, what we find is that they are *weighted differently*. This concept is key to understanding how to analyze both verbal and nonverbal communication together.

To explain this, let us look at a hypothetical situation:

You are on a first date. Not knowing too much about the person you are seeing, you pick what you think is a nice restaurant. It is better than nice. It is filled with people clothed in expensive wear, eating fancy food, while surrounded by valuable paintings and decor. Surely this will impress your date. You have a conversation with each other while eating your food. You ask if the food is nice. Your date says it is. You ask if they are having a lovely time. They say they are. Why then, do you have this sinking feeling that they are unhappy and that there will never be a second date?

The answer is that your date has weighted their verbal and nonverbal communication differently. Verbally, they are saying all the right things, most probably because they do not want to offend. All of their concentration then has gone towards verbally reassuring you. They have prioritized or *weighted* this form of communication to negotiate what is a problematic social exchange. But while they concentrate on their verbal communication, this has allowed their conscious efforts to control their nonverbal communication to slip. Their posture is tense, they do not engage their hands at all, no affectionate movements, and in fact, their entire physical demeanor is of someone who cannot wait to get the date over.

What we see here, is that by placing higher psychological *weight* on verbalizing things, this causes internal distraction. So, the limbic system is producing negative emotions that filter through to our body language and facial expressions.

The takeaway here is that nonverbal communication is often *enhanced* or stronger when a person is also speaking at the same time. As a species, we are not very good at multitasking psychologically. It creates an excellent opportunity for those who understand how to read people, to truly gauge how they feel when those defensive walls come down.

Chapter 5
Nonverbal Behavior of the Arms

Now that we understand the basics of where nonverbal communication comes from, its place alongside verbal communication, and how to analyze a person's body language, etc., we can now learn about specific gestures, postures, and expressions. These will help you predict and understand a person's thoughts and goals. The following chapters will focus on the human body and how each region of it is used to communicate information. In this chapter, we begin with analyzing nonverbal behavior of the arms.

How to Analyze People Through Nonverbal Behavior of the Arms

The arms always depict some sort of nonverbal internal emotion or thought. It manifests as either a *posture* or a *gesture*. When analyzing the position of the arms, look for how the arms are held almost still. It could be in an open stance (arms extended out welcomingly) or a closed posture (arms folded defensively). When you analyze the gestures, look for how the arms move around. We'll touch more on that in the next chapter about hand gestures, as they are usually apparent at the same time.

Defensive Arm Displays

We have used the example of the arms folded in front of the body several times so far, and this is because it is one of the most common postures in nonverbal body language. It's also often one of the easiest to interpret. As we mentioned earlier, the arms are crossed in front of the stomach, which is a vulnerable area due to only being partially protected by the rib cage. It then is often seen as a protective stance. It is exhibited usually for one or more of the following reasons:

- Feeling defensive at what is being accused or said. It could merely be disagreeing with the content of a significant other's speech.

- Feeling nervous or anxious. By crossing the arms, not only is a person protecting themselves, but they are also trying to hide and not be noticed.

- The person is feeling comfortable, and folding their arms is the most comfortable position for them to take at that time.

Notice how the last point disagrees with the first two. You must look for other nonverbal signs to either support or refute your initial interpretation. An example would be if the person were sitting down and locking their ankles together or crossing their feet. It is commonly seen with folded arms and is highly correlated with a defensive or negative attitude. Lastly, look for what the hands are doing alongside the folded arms. If they are clenched, this represents even more tension in the body and their attitude.

Arm Withdrawal

If you notice a person's arms being pulled inward towards their body, this can mean that they disagree with what you are saying, or even with who you are as a person. It can also convey disgust and anger. It can also represent apathy and a desire to withdraw from a conversation or situation. This movement can be significant, but it can also be subtle. Keep an eye out for anyone withdrawing their arms towards their body even slightly.

Arm withdrawal is often presented alongside leaning away from the speaker, facing away from them, or disgusted and bored postures and facial expressions. In some instances, the offending person does not even need to speak to cause this defensive behavior.

Arms Freeze Display

We naturally communicate with our arms and hands. These are among the most common gestures, and so movement in the arms is a continual way of communication. However, in some specific circumstances, these movements can halt. The arms

49

become entirely still, often staying lifeless at the side of the body, but they can also freeze into other postures. This "Arm Freezing", is usually a sign that something is amiss. Remember earlier, we talked about the fight, flight, and freeze response? Arm freezing is the product of the freeze component. We tend to stay very still naturally when we believe there is a threat nearby. It is a way to avoid detection by dangerous human beings or animals. In this sense, then, arm freezing is usually a bad sign that a person doesn't just feel defensive, but that they feel *threatened*.

If someone presents this behavior, it could mean that they are overwhelmed with stress or that they feel ideologically or personally threatened by something or someone nearby. It is essential to recognize this behavior and try to set the person at ease if their arm freezing seems disproportionate.

The Self-Hug

Remember the adapters we discussed in an earlier chapter? How we have certain nonverbal behaviors which are designed to calm or vent a painful internal emotion? A self-hug is an excellent example of this. It can be seen when a person wraps their arms around the front of their body and then holds the outside of the opposite arm. There can sometimes be a rubbing or hugging motion as well. It is an adapter to make a person feel better if they are stressed. The stress can be slight or more pronounced.

We often naturally use this posture when preparing for a difficult situation like hearing bad news or waiting to face an exam. Caution should be taken; however, self-hugging can also mean a person is cold. Again, look for other nonverbal and verbal signs which will help you decode this behavior.

Territorial Arms Displays

The arms can be used to mark off territory. It can be a space or even a person. It is common to see partners with their arms around each other or arms locked together in public places. While this can be purely affectionate, it can also be a way to say to others, *"this is my mate."* Of course, we do not like to think of people as objects, but we have to remember how impulsive our brains can be. We are, after all, part ape, and those brain impulses are still competing alongside our humanity and even-mindedness. An example of this would be seeing your partner talking to someone attractive and then walking up and smiling while putting your arm around your partner. It is a definitive territorial behavior.

When marking off territory with the arms, you may also see people stretch out or lean against something with their arm or elbow. It is a way to say *"this is mine."* You might also see yawning used as an adapter in some situations, allowing a person to stretch their arms out around them. We accept that someone might stretch for comfort while yawning, but it is also often used to establish personal space. Moving the arms around, you can also mean that you want to be isolated and left alone.

Welcoming Arm Movements

We have focused heavily on adverse arm movements and postures, but the arms can also be used to say positive things. When arms are outstretched in front of a person, especially in a Y formation, this represents a hugging motion. Likewise, when a person opens up their body during conversation and the arms part to show their torso, this is a sign that they are responding to what is being said and welcoming of it. It can also be a sign of developing trust.

Chapter 6
Nonverbal Behavior of Hands and Palms

"I talk with my hands a lot." How often have you heard someone say something similar to this? When people think of nonverbal communication, they often think of hand gestures because we use them so often. When analyzing a person's nonverbal communication, these gestures are of paramount importance.

How to Analyze People Via the Nonverbal Behavior of Their hands and Palms

We mentioned briefly in chapter 4 when comparing nonverbal and verbal communications, that body language especially tends to be much slower than speech because no words are used. However, of all the types of nonverbal communication, hand gestures are easily the fastest. While they cannot change meaning as quickly or convey the same nuance as speech, they can still communicate ideas and internal drives at speed.

What this means for analysis is that you must think quickly through what a gesture truly means. It takes practice as it requires a speed of thought and decoding, which usually lies dormant within each of us. There are some shortcuts; however, one of the most powerful is to think of what hands are often used for - to point at things. The movement of the hands can, therefore, subtly point in the direction of meaning.

How Hand Movements Boost Your Credibility and Persuasiveness

As infants, one of the first ways we learn to communicate with other human beings truly is through hand gestures. It can be pointing at something or waving hello. It can also be showing something being held, offering it up to a parent. Due to this early adoption of nonverbal hand communication, we instinctively put weight on hand gestures, especially when it comes to persuasiveness and credibility. We naturally use our hands to beckon someone to come closer, which is one of the most persuasive gestures a person can make. We can also show our hands palm up and open, signifying that there is no danger - no clenched fist and no weapon in hand. In this way, hand gestures are so crucial to creating persuasiveness.

Credibility is also a factor. To establish credibility through nonverbal communication, a person must at least seem sincere, even if they are not. As hand gestures are so primal, when they are backed up by other postures and gestures which support the gesture, they can establish a broad sense of credibility and trust.

Watch Out for Those Who Hide Their Hands!

Hand gestures are so fundamental to the way we communicate that it can be challenging to control what we are saying through them ultimately. If we want to hide information about ourselves and our thoughts, then one strategy is to hide the hands. We often do not think about this consciously; it just feels right, like an adapter. However, when people put their hands in their pockets, fold them tightly under their arms so they cannot move, or clench their fists together, they are instinctively trying to hide what their hands *want* to say.

While hand hiding is often associated with deception, it can also be done to convey passivity or submissiveness. The image of a school child with their hands in their pockets as a teacher reprimands them is more in line with this. Look for other signs of passivity such as hunched shoulders, lounging, and staring at the ground to see if this holds.

Hand Gestures Speak Volumes

Let us look at a few common hand gestures. These are:

Steepling: This is when the fingertips of both hands push up against each other. It is absolutely a power play. It conveys thinking, but not just that, *intellect*. Knowledge is power, and if a person can convince others that they are wise and contemplative, then they are more likely to be heard. Steepling can also be used to show a relaxed yet authoritative state under challenging circumstances. A leadership move that says, *"I have the wisdom to solve this problem."*

Hands-on Hips: Also known as "hands akimbo", this gesture brings the arms into play. When the hands are placed on the hips, the elbows of each arm naturally point outwards. It takes up space, and deliberately so. It is a form of dominance behavior showing that a person is in control of their area. It also makes a person seem more significant and more imposing, which again can be critical during power plays. Sometimes it can backfire and seem condescending and judgmental.

Hand Wringing: This involves clasping one hand over the other. It can be done tightly or loosely, and the distinction is essential. If it is done tightly, then this suggests worry and stress, if it is done lightly, then it can be similar to hand steepling. Most of the time, it is used to either calm others by saying *"I'm not a threat"*, or to make people feel sorry and concerned for someone. In some instances, this can be used deceptively, so look out for other manipulative nonverbal and verbal cues.

Analyze People Through Their Handshakes - The Power of the Handshake

Touching is a massive aspect of nonverbal communication, though as cultural changes reinterpret all forms of physical touch as invasive, this may change over time. However, one way of touching which remains constant in many cultures is the handshake. The handshake is often used to greet or say goodbye - but it does so much more than this. An overly firm handshake can imply that a person is trying to appear either dominant or physically virile. It is all about conveying confidence, which is why a firm handshake is often promoted in business circles.

It is essential to note the position of the palms and what that suggests. If someone shakes hands with their palm down on top of the other person's, this is to show superiority. Likewise, when the palm is up, it can denote submissiveness. Most people will shake hands with their palms parallel to each other - this promotes a feeling of equality; however, the pressure of the handshake can still betray a sense of dominance. Think about what the palm orientation truly means for any relationship:

- Palm Down: A person *wants* to dominate you.
- Palm Up: A person *wants* to be dominated.
- Palms Parallel: Both people seek an equal relationship.

Other nonverbal signs of dominance may also occur when someone tries to pull a person's hand towards them (note, in some circumstances, this might just be over-exuberance and happiness at seeing someone). They may also smile widely and look a person in the eye.

Breaking a dominant handshake can be tricky. Techniques include:

Double Hander: Offer your hand palm up, then after the shake commences, bring your free hand down on top of the handshake. Then, place some light pressure with both hands to ensure that your palms stay parallel and not dominant or submissive.

Foot change: If you are right-handed, step forward with your left foot. It will create a stance that is challenging to dominate as it is unusual; it also nullifies the dominant handshake of the other person who will often try to step forward into your personal space.

Offensive Hand Displays

Lastly, let us talk briefly about aggressive hand displays. There is a lot of cultural difference when it comes to establishing what is offensive and what is not. It shows that there is a strong environmental aspect to how people attribute meaning to gestures. It is essential to learn about cultural differences and apply this to your decoding of nonverbal behaviors.

Some offensive hand displays do seem to be almost universal such as flicking the chin, whereby placing the back of the hand underneath the chin and then flicking the hand forward is generally seen as an offensive, frustrated, angry gesture. However, there are some nuances to it, depending on location.

Some common western hand gestures can seem subtle but be offensive elsewhere, such as the thumbs up "okay" signal. It can mean "up yours" in other countries, even somewhere like Australia, which is heavily culturally influenced by America and Europe. Going through all the different perturbations of cultural hand gesture differences is beyond the scope of this book. Still, it is a good idea to research these differences should you be traveling abroad to avoid offending.

Chapter 7
Nonverbal Behavior of the Legs and Feet

W e naturally spend so much time observing all nonverbal communication above the waist that we often overlook the importance of the legs and feet in body language. Both have a lot to say, and, when combined with the other parts of the body, can be used expertly to understand and predict behavior.

How to Analyze People Through Nonverbal Behaviors of the Legs

When analyzing the body language of the legs and feet, it is essential to recognize why internal feelings and thoughts manifest through them. Hand gestures are seen naturally as a communicative medium. It is because we write words with them, paint with them, clap or shoo away someone with them - they are inherently understood on a human level as being used for

61

communication. We do not think about the legs and feet in the same way. They are for walking, kicking, and jumping - so why should we pay attention to them?

It is precise *because* we overlook the legs and feet that we should pay attention to them. When trying to psychologically control our speech, hand gestures, trunk posture, facial expressions, and eye gestures, we put so many cognitive resources towards them, that we forget ourselves about our legs and feet as ways to communicate. That makes them pretty unique. It means that our subconscious or *true* feelings are presented through them for the most part rather than deception.

That is a powerful thing to know when analyzing behavior. With that knowledge, you can decode a person's thoughts through how they use their legs and feet. To do so, pay attention to:

- Gait or stance
- Feet position
- Crossing or locking of legs and ankles
- Fidgeting feet and leg movement

Types of Leg and Feet Displays

There are several ways in which we display our legs and feet, subconsciously (and occasionally consciously) conveying our internal psychology through them. Some of the most important ones to look out for are:

Leg Crossing: Both men and women cross their legs. It can be similar to when the arms are crossed, protecting vulnerable parts of the body and being closed off. It is especially important when interpreting possible sexual thoughts. However, the most critical component is not the way the legs are crossed, but rather where they are pointing. When someone crosses their legs, but the legs or feet naturally point towards a person that conveys the opposite feeling - this is an open gesture, which means a person is willing to listen.

Ankle Crossing: When the feet cross over each other, and the arms are crossed, this "locking" posture is usually defensive. However, when the ankles are crossed, and the legs are splayed, this conveys a relaxed state.

Leg Splaying: Speaking of leg splaying, if crossed legs can imply a closed-off attitude when the legs are either parted widely (most commonly in men) or straightened out in a Y position when sitting, this conveys relaxation. However, it can also display a lack of care for how others perceive the person doing the leg splaying, which can imply recklessness. This takes up unnecessary space and can also be seen as an aggressive territorial claim.

Shaking or Wiggling: An extremely common stress adapter is leg shaking or feet wiggling. Many people are unaware they are even doing it. It implies anxiety of some kind, with the movements taking the mind away from those thoughts and calming the limbic system. It can also suggest irritation.

Foot Tapping: Subtly different from foot wiggling, the rhythmic tapping of the foot can, of course, simply mean someone is enjoying the pulse of the music. However, it can also mean that a person is feeling impatient and anxious to get moving.

Stride: Most feet and leg displays involve sitting down, but a pace while walking can tell us a lot about someone's state of mind. If the stride is stable and not overly hurried, then the person is feeling confident. If the pace is erratic and uncertain, then there is anxiety there, most probably some sort of social worry about how others perceive the walker.

Defensive Leg Displays: Keeping the knees clamped tightly together can be a dead giveaway that a person is feeling defensive. Of course, it can also be because a person is wearing a skirt, so always be mindful of how the context affects interpretation.

Hand Display and Leg Display Combinations

It is essential to be aware of specific hand displays that can be combined with leg displays, altering their meaning. It usually involves the touching of the legs in some way. When we talked about adapters, we mentioned hand cleansing, which is when a person rubs their hands on their thighs. It can alter how we perceive the leg position. For example, one ankle may be resting on the other thigh, creating an open, relaxed stance. However, when hand cleansing is introduced, this shows that there is some anxiety and that the leg position is only part of the picture. Likewise, someone could be sitting looking relaxed with their arms by their sides, but the legs are tightly crossed. Again, this gives us something to ponder. We must then look for other nonverbal cues that would allow us to weigh the two behaviors, giving us a better chance to figure out which one is most prevalent and current in the person's mind. Any self-touching of the legs can be interpreted as representing anxiety, even knee clasping when both hands are clasping one or both knees.

Chapter 8
Nonverbal Behavior of the Face

I f hand gestures are some of the fastest-changing nonverbal behaviors, then facial expressions are the most complex. Of course, facial expressions change over time, though not as quickly as hand gestures. What is most challenging about analyzing them is that they can be so nuanced. A small flicker of a look can appear for a moment - what did it mean? Was that an underlying thought bubbling to the surface? A momentary daydream? Facial expressions in their purest forms are simplistic, but it is how we, as human beings, mix possible combinations, which makes them so subtle at times.

How to Analyze People Through the Nonverbal Behavior of the Face

Facial expressions can be *proactive* or *reactive*. It is through understanding this distinction that you will have

67

a better success rate when analyzing key expression attributes. Dynamic facial expressions occur when they are "sent" out to be received. For example, if someone were to tell you a funny story and they start laughing and smiling as they are saying it - that's a proactive facial expression. It is intended to be received, and usually comes in tandem with a speech that is directed at another person. Do not mistake this for always being conscious of nonverbal communication. It is not. Sometimes a person chooses to smile while talking, but at other times the smile will come through subconsciously. What is essential here is to recognize that the facial expression is being broadcast as part of a message.

Reactive expressions happen when a person is receiving and responding to information. Taking the above example, although the person telling you the funny story is laughing, you start to frown. Why? Because you find the joke to be in poor taste. It again could be an instinctive reaction or one you deliberately broadcast, but what makes it reactive is that the facial expression is in *response* to something.

Think about these two broad categories of facial expressions as you analyze a person's behavior. Are they responding or sending? If they are sending out a facial expression while talking, then this is more likely to be what they *want* to be perceived. That does not mean it is accurate. If they are responding, then it is more likely that it is an instinctual response and, therefore, more representative of what is going on in their mind.

Of course, there are ifs, buts, and maybes surrounding these two categories. Sometimes a person can be sending out reactive expressions while talking because they are responding to their own emotions and how their communication is being received. In this way, all we can say about *reactive* and *proactive* expressions is that they tend to be presented when switching between receiving and sending messages.

What are Micro Expressions?

When we mentioned the nuance of facial expressions and how subtle they can be, we were referring to *micro expressions*. These are small movements of the face that reveal the true feelings and thoughts of a person. They are usually involuntary and great examples of emotional impulses from the limbic system pushing past an individual's defenses to being revealed to the outside world.

Facial expressions can be faked (more on that below). However, micro expressions are much more difficult to fake because of their involuntary nature. There are seven established micro-expressions, and each of them is connected to deep, visceral emotion. Be vigilant for each when analyzing someone. These micro-expressions are:

Surprise: This manifests itself as having raised eyebrows, wrinkled brow, wide-open eyes, and often the jaw-dropping full and showing teeth. The surprise is relatively ambiguous as it can be either a negative response or a positive response.

Hate: Also referred to as contempt, it often presents itself with one side of the mouth raised. There can also be a furrowed brow, but hatred is often accompanied by a blank or apathetic expression.

Sadness: This emotion filters through onto the face with the lips curled down at the sides and a furrowed brow, which arches upward in the middle creating vertical and horizontal lines. The cheeks and muscles around the eyes can be tensed.

Happiness: When a moment of joy flickers across the face, it presents with no wrinkled brow, a smile, raised cheeks, and crow's feet at the sides of the eyes.

Disgust: This has a surprise component, though mixed with disgust. It manifests on the face with raised upper eyelids, curled upper lip with nose wrinkled, and the cheeks raised. It can also present with a furrowed brow, and the corners of the mouth curved downwards.

Anger: This presents itself with eyebrows lowering and furled in the middle. Often vertical lines appear between the eyebrows. Lower lids tense up and raise slightly. Pursed lips. Flaring nostrils. Gritting teeth. A focused stare, and also tilting of the head slightly downward, occasionally upward.

Fear: Perhaps the most instinctive emotion of all. It manifests as raised eyebrows that are curling towards each other in the middle of the brow—which causes the forehead to become wrinkled. As a surprise, the eyes are quite wide, but the lower lids do not pull down as much.

The mouth will open with the chin, sometimes pulling in towards the chest.

Sometimes these micro-expressions can be present at the same time or in close proximately, so stay alert to such changes should they occur.

Facial Expressions can be Faked!

We have mentioned the importance of deception in nonverbal communication. It is common practice for a deceptive individual to use facial expressions to fake communication or hide what they are thinking. However, as they are so intuitive, only the most seasoned (and sometimes sociopathic) can fake micro-expressions realistically.

That being said, it is essential to keep an eye out for common signs of deception. For example, someone who is smiling widely with their mouth, but their eyelids remain static, is most probably not that happy. Look for combinations of competing for micro expressions. If you see someone smile, but their brow is furrowed as if disgusted, you will see the conflict between what they are trying to show you and what they are thinking.

Isolated Nonverbal Expressions

As well as micro-expressions, there are several expressions and states which can be isolated to parts of the face. These can also help you to detect deception, but can also reinforce your interpretation of another nonverbal cue. Stay aware of:

Eye Gestures: Just as the hands can make gestures conveying meaning, the eyes can too. Looking away and to the side, while talking, can mean deception as the person is trying to think through what they are saying, but it can also mean the person is trying to remember something. Too much eye contact seems unnatural, and again if someone is never breaking their stare, deception or an attempt at domination is likely. Staring at the ground or focusing on the hands can also be an adapter to alleviate nervousness. A glazed look shows disinterest or daydreaming. Even the dilation of the pupils can tell us something, with overly dilated eyes linked to forms of deception and arousal.

Glasses and Makeup: Remember that how the body interacts with the environment can contain vital clues about intent and desires. If a person wears glasses, for example, they can use these in a way which shows concentration (taking the glasses off and putting one of the arms in the mouth), or dislike (looking over the top of the glasses with the head tilted down). Likewise, makeup can be used to infer a state of mind or personality type (more on personality types in Chapter 9). Makeup, which draws attention to the mouth and eyes are often misread as purely to attract a mate, but they are commonly used to portray confidence. In some circumstances, makeup can be an adapter of sorts to help reduce insecurity. The style of makeup used can also tell us how the individual feels about a specific situation in some circumstances (professional vs. personal).

The Lips: We have mentioned how the lips can convey information above. They can smile when happy or relaxed, the corners can point down when sad or disgusted, and they can tense up or become pursed when stressed or worried.

Nose Flare Displays: Our nostrils flare to take in more air, and this often occurs when our pulse rate quickens. It can be due to anger or arousal.

Furrowed Forehead Display: The eyebrows convey much about how a person is feeling. What is fascinating about them is that with just a small alteration, they can appear to express an opposing emotion. When frowning, the eyebrows draw together, and this brings the forehead into play. When this happens in tandem, we can see annoyance, anger, or deep concentration.

Blushing and Blanching: Blushing has long been associated with feeling embarrassment or feeling attracted to someone. One theory behind the use of blush makeup is that it mimics this signal and therefore attracts people towards it. However, blushing can mean anxiety or a quickening pulse as the capillaries in the face open up. It can also be the case that a person has social worries about blushing, and this exacerbates the issue. It can also be a defensive reaction when deceiving someone. However, some individuals simply have a strong flush response, and that should not be read into much.

Smiles and Laughter: The World's Most Irresistible Gestures

Laughter and smiling are both powerful communicators. As you no doubt, realize by now, they are, like most nonverbal cues, capable of being presented consciously and subconsciously. What is so fascinating about the smile is that it is also the most common means of deception. The main reason it is used for is a fraud because people are naturally treated more positively when they smile, in some cases, even receiving more lenient sentences in the courts. It is called the smile leniency effect, and it is why lying through smiling is so commonly attempted.

It is not always easy to spot, but fake smiles can be identified by:

A Lack of Closed Eyes: Smiling brings about changes in the upper face. This includes the eyelids narrowing. If the eyes are wide or cold looking, then the smile is only skin deep.

No Crow's Feet: The orbicularis oculi muscle creates wrinkles around the eyes when we smile. However, when someone is faking a smile, this muscle often does not engage.

Showing Lower Teeth: When someone fakes a smile, they sometimes show their lower teeth. When we smile naturally, the zygomatic major muscle group pulls the smile upward, which means the bottom teeth should fully or partially obscure the lips. If you can see a lot of the lower teeth, this may suggest deception.

Smiles come in many shapes and sizes, but psychologists have identified five main types. By being able to differentiate between them, it is possible to become a far more skillful reader of facial expressions. The five smile types are:

1. **The Seductive Smile**: This smile is used to either gain favor or signal attraction. It involves a subtle smile but with extended direct eye contact and then a slow glancing away. It also includes submissive head tilting to the side or downward.

2. **Sarcastic Smile**: Here, the mouth is upturned as though happy. Sometimes the mouth is a crooked smirk, and there is always a look of mocking disbelief or disdain in the eyes.

3. **Fake Smile**: We've covered this one extensively.

4. **Uncomfortable Smile**: This smile is usually born out of nervousness. It is often a way to satisfy someone who has said something you do not agree with, but you do not want to get into a confrontation about it. The smile is often closed-lipped, and the eyebrows raise slightly and curl up in the center.

5. **Duchenne Smile**: Coined by psychologist Paul Ekman, this smile is the real deal - it expresses real

happiness. It is the polar opposite of a fake laugh complete with narrowing eyelids, crow's feet, with the cheeks raised.

Part Three

Personality Traits

Chapter 9
What is Personality?

In our final two chapters, we are going to explore personality and its traits. It is essential for analyzing someone through their verbal and nonverbal communication. The reason is that established personality traits can be used to fill in missing data with a reasonable degree of accuracy. By using what you have learned in analyzing behavior, you can then compare your interpretations with personality categories. When you believe there is a good fit, you can use those categories to delve deeper and glean ever more meaningful insight into the person you are observing and, perhaps, even yourself.

How is Personality Defined?

When we think about our personalities, we often believe that our personality is the entirety of our mental being. It is who we are - our memories, our experiences, and our beliefs. It is correct in a way; however, personality is something that is projected. It is not just an internal

79

process but heavily defined by our actions and words. Our character is deeply affected by our experiences, but it is also affected by our genetics. The critical missing component here is choice. If you believe in free will, then the culmination of your personality is when you take all of those experiences and impulses and then choose which ones to act out. If you do not believe in free will, then personality can be seen as the end product of a long causal chain of experiences that produces a specific outcome - our behavior.

Personality is, therefore, our unique blend of influences, impulses, and decisions. There is only one you.

Reading People Through Personality Traits

What makes personality so crucial in reading people is that it tends to be relatively stable over long periods. It will change through experience, but those changes are usually gradual unless sparked by significant trauma. Because those changes are gradual, and also because for many personality traits can even last a lifetime, it is a great predictor of future behavior. It is also an effective way to understand how and why a person thinks and behaves the way they do, by understanding a person's personality, we often appreciate their history and how it led to the person they are today.

How do we "read" personality effectively? Well, much of what you have learned in this book will help with that. However, several personality categories have been discovered by psychologists over the last 150 years. Stringent psychometric testing and observations have produced personality traits that are seen throughout the human population again and again. These traits can be seen as attributes.

By knowing the key attributes of these personality traits, you will be able to apply what you know about them to those you observe quickly.

The Big 5 Factors That Determine Different Personality Traits

Personality is forged from many and varied influences. However, the five most important factors which contribute to personality traits are:

1. **Conscientiousness**: A measure of how thoughtful a person is to others. It includes reasonable impulse control and a tendency for organization.

2. **Extraversion**: How socially outgoing is a person. Involves aspects like sociability, assertiveness, and how communicative they are about their emotions.

3. **Agreeableness**: How well you interact with others. Includes altruism, kindness, affection, and other behaviors considered prosocial.

4. **Neuroticism**: Negative and disruptive emotions. It involves sadness, irritability, anxiety, and emotional instability.

5. **Openness**: How open a person is to new experiences. It includes creativity and a call to adventure.

Positive personality traits are any characteristics that positively affect the individual's sense of wellbeing, his or her interactions with others, and their success in achieving the goals they set for themselves. Negative personality traits are destructive to relationships, goals, and how a person is perceived.

In psychology, negative personality traits can be so affecting that they are classified as *personality disorders*. These disorders are pathological in a sense and run the gamut from compulsive liars to serial killers.

How Each Personality Trait Communicates

Look again at the Big Five. These traits have a significant impact on the type of personality a person has. They also produce different behaviors and thus communicate differently. The way a trait communicates is going to govern much of the nonverbal and verbal communications a person uses. If someone scores high on agreeableness, their body language may be more open and welcoming. Conversely, if a person scores higher on neuroticism, they will present more anxious, negative behaviors, and will use more adapters to calm them.

By studying the Big Five traits, you will be able to gauge the likelihood of behaviors you have not seen from a person yet. If someone is kind and uses nurturing body language, there is a good chance that they will be altruistic, too. If someone has outwardly aggressive and narcissistic nonverbal and verbal cues, then you might conclude that they score low on conscientiousness, and so are probably unlikely to have reasonable impulse control and thus may be reckless in the future.

The Big 5 acts as a funnel for your analytical ability to read people, bringing with its further insight into personality traits, helping you understand people more effectively.

Chapter 10
Can You Change Your Personality?

Now that you know about nonverbal and verbal communications, as well as personality traits that correlate with them and provide greater insight into others, let us conclude our journey with some introspection. Let us use what we know as an instrument of self-improvement.

Is Personality Permanent?

Can a person truly change? Psychologists and philosophers have asked this question for thousands of years. What we now know in the modern age is that the human brain's most significant advantage is its *neuroplasticity*. The mind can rewire, to create new connections between neurons as it learns new skills and perspectives. Up until recently, we also thought that once the brain matured at around 25 years of age, that it produced no new neurons. We now know that *neurogenesis*, the process of neuron creation can still happen later in life. All of this comes together to provide us with hope.

Every one of us can change as individuals. Personality is deep-rooted in our experiences and genetics, but our intention can drive it. Our consciousness, which makes decisions and guides us through life, can decide to turn over a new leaf, to strive for a change which will profoundly impact our lives. That consciousness is what we truly are, whether you believe it is the product of the brain or something immaterial. Regardless, we can each of us decide at any age to turn our lives around for the better.

What you have learned throughout this chapter is how to understand personality and behavior. You now know that your personality can be analyzed in the same way.

Defining your Personality

Take time now to observe your behavior. Think of your motivations. What impulse or feelings drive you to carry out your actions? Are you happy with these impulses and choices? Think about the Big Five Factors of Personality - how do they apply to you? Which traits do you have, and which do you lack?

You can also try out some psychological surveys such as the Sixteen Personality Factor Questionnaire self-report test, which will give you a great indicator of which traits dominate your personality.

Once you have a good idea of your personality traits, is there anything you would like to change? For most of us, the answer is always a resounding *"yes."*

How Do I Create My Personality?

Changing your personality should be about making the traits you find most admirable and worthwhile part of who you are at a fundamental level. It does not happen overnight. It takes time. But you can do this through:

Changing Your State of Mind: Our outlook or state of mind affects everything we do, good and bad. If we feel positive, the world is a good place. If we think negatively, this can make every aspect of life feel like a chore. Changing your state of mind to one who cultivates positivity and wants to make proactive changes to your personality can be achieved. Meditation, exercise, proper nutrition, good sleep, and a gratitude journal can all facilitate this change.

Making Small Changes: When it comes to habit building and achievement, all the psychological data points to small, consistent changes being the key. If we try to change too much at once, we become overloaded and fail. Small steps lead to great journeys.

Your personality can be a beacon in the night for all those around you. By using what you have learned to boost your personality and meet the needs of others through your understanding of their verbal and nonverbal communications, you can be a force for good in the world. Make your personality your ideal self, and you will have greater success in your life.

Conclusion

We are now at the end of our journey. You have learned much already about human communication and personality, and how to use this to read and understand those around you. You have learned that through understanding the psychological motives of people through their personality traits, you can negotiate and interact with people more effectively. And finally, you know how to apply these lessons to your own life to create the personality you genuinely desire.

Understanding and developing nonverbal reading skills takes time, insight, and knowledge. Build on what you have learned. Keep reading, and your ability to resonate deeply with your fellow human beings and understand their needs will expand until you indeed are a master of analyzing those around you.

What Did You Think of How to Read Anyone Instantly?

First of all, thank you for purchasing this book, How to Read Anyone Instantly. I know you could have picked any number of books to read, but you picked this book and for that I am extremely grateful.

I hope you found it informative and valuable and wish you all the best in taking your first steps in analyzing people. I would really appreciate it if you could share this book with your friends and family by posting to **Facebook** and **Twitter**.

If you enjoyed this book and found some benefit in reading this, I'd like to also hear from you and hope that you could take some time to post an honest review on Amazon. I value my readers feedback as gaining exposure as an independent author relies mostly on word of mouth reviews and this would greatly improve my writing craft for future projects and make this book even better. So, if you have the time and inclination, it would be much appreciated.

If you'd like to leave a review, all you have to do is scan the below QR Code and away you go.

About the Author

Daniel Glanville studied a Master's degree in Psychology and currently lives in Buckinghamshire, United Kingdom. He enjoys to document his personal findings and experiences with a view to help people better understand and handle certain situations that are proving challenging to deal with. He has been captivated by the notion of human interaction, behavior and communication since he was a young boy and dedicates his spare time to writing self-development books. He offers people an opportunity to apply his simple and straightforward strategies to live a better quality of life.

David has a love for journaling, painting open landscapes and people watching. He enjoys hosting small gatherings with friends and considers himself quite the wine tasting expert.

Printed by Amazon Italia Logistica S.r.l.
Torrazza Piemonte (TO), Italy

16442844R00057